INVENTORS & INVENTIONS

RADIOLOGY

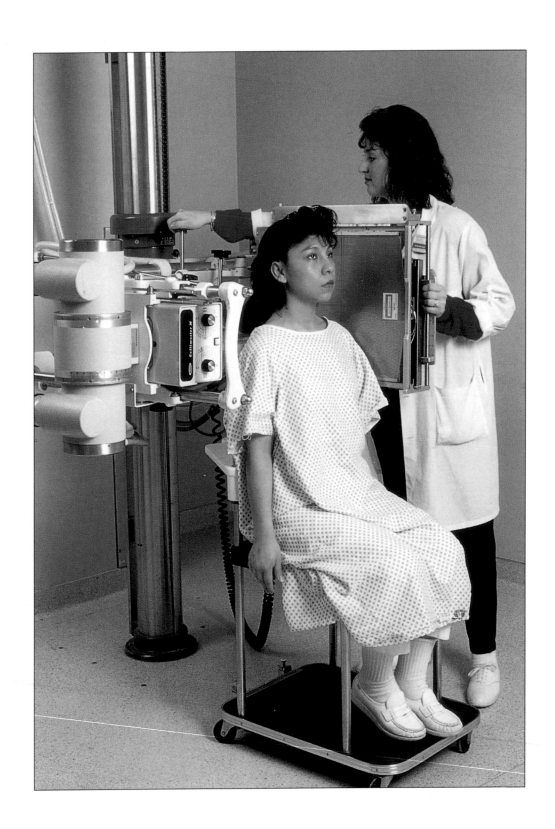

INVENTORS & INVENTIONS

RADIOLOGY

KATHY WINKLER

BENCHMARK BOOKS

MARSHALL CAVENDISH
NEW YORK

Benchmark Books
Marshall Cavendish Corporation
99 White Plains Road
Tarrytown, New York 10591-9001

©Marshall Cavendish Corporation, 1996

Series created by The Creative Publishing Company

Library of Congress Cataloging-in-Publication Data

Winkler, Kathy.
    Radiology / Kathy Winkler.
        p.   cm. -- (Inventors & inventions)
    Includes index.
    Summary: An overview of the science of radiology, from Roentgen's
discovery of the x-ray to the evolving uses of radiology in medicine and industry.
    ISBN 0-7614-0075-3 (lib. bdg.)
    1. Radiology, Medical--Juvenile literature.   2. Radiology-
-Juvenile literature.   [1. Radiology, Medical.]   I. Title.
II. Series.
R695.W56   1996
616.07'57--dc20   95-41575
                                        CIP
                                        AC

Printed in Hong Kong

Acknowledgments

Technical Consultant: Steven L. Barnicki, Ph.D.
Illustration on page 30 by Julian Baker

The publishers would like to thank the following for their permission to reproduce photographs:
Mary Evans/Fawcett Library, (28); Hulton Deutsch, (19, 21); Juan del Regato, (27, 48, 49); Science Photo Library Ltd., (10, Tim Beddow cover, Custom Medical Stock Photo frontispiece, Chris Bjornberg 6, Susan Leavines 7, Dr. Jeremy Burgess 8, Philippe Plailly/Eurelios 9, J-L Charmet 17, 25, BSIP Boucharlat 32, BSIP VEM 33, BSIP, S&I 34, Erik Hildebrandt 35, Philippe Plailly/Eurelios 36, Alexander Tsiaras 37, Chris Priest 39, Philippe Plailly 42, Simon Fraser 43, Alexander Tsiaras 45, Martin Dohrn 47, Will & Deni McIntyre 50, Alexander Tsiaras 51, James King-Holmes/OCMS 52, Metropolitan Museum & Brookhaven National Laboratory 53l, Brookhaven National Laboratory 53r, Alexander Tsiaras 55, Philippe Plailly/Eurelios 56, Alexander Tsiaras 57, John Greim 58, Hank Morgan 59); Science & Society Picture Library, (12, 13); UPI/Bettmann, (14, 15, 18, 22, 31, 40, 41).

(Cover) Using a hand-held ultrasound scanner, a technician scans a patient's neck. An image of the scanned area can be seen on the monitor.

(Frontispiece) A patient prepares to undergo a neck x-ray. The x-ray source is to her right, and the x-ray film, held by the radiographer, is to her left.

Contents

Chapter 1
Looking Inside the Body

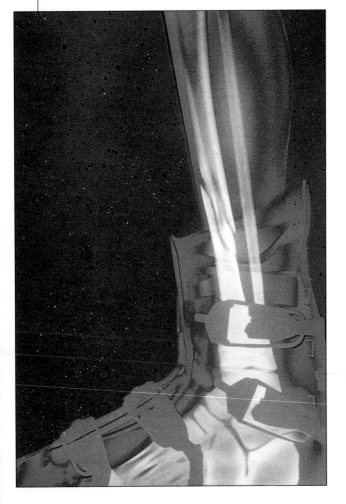

A modern x-ray of a foot, taken while it is still inside a ski boot. The x-ray shows that the tibia, the larger of the two bones in the lower leg, has a multiple fracture. A computer has colored the image to make the details clearer.

Jenny stood in the crisp winter air, checking out the ski run below. With a shove, she was off. Snow-covered pines flashed by and sunshine sparkled on the snow. What Jenny didn't know was that just ahead lay a patch of rough ice, covered by a thin layer of glittering snow. She heard the grind of ski on ice and landed hard; her leg gave a sharp *crack* as the lower bone split deep inside.

Ski Patrollers, well trained in first aid, strapped Jenny to an immobilizing board. Then, they took her down the hill on a big sled. It certainly wasn't the way Jenny had planned to come down!

"Well, young lady," said the white-coated doctor at a nearby hospital. "Looks like you've really done a number on your leg. I think we'd better get a picture of that!"

The doctor needed to know what had happened inside Jenny's leg before planning what to do about it. Had a bone broken? Which one? Where? How bad was the break? Were the two broken ends in line or did they have to be moved together?

An x-ray would give the answers. An x-ray technician had Jenny lie on a table under a modern version of the x-ray tube first developed in the 1890s. The machine sent its rays through her leg, leaving an image on the film. The result, after developing, was a "picture" of Jenny's leg, clearly showing the break.

Most people have an x-ray at some point in their lives. They're very common when someone is injured, when a doctor suspects a certain disease, or as part of a dental checkup.

Many people think of an x-ray as what Jenny had done on her leg, but there are actually three major ways of using x-rays, all part of the broader scientific field called *radiology*. In addition, there are also several specialized types of radiology, including using radiology to treat disease, which we will cover in a later chapter. For now, let's look at the three basic types.

Radiography, Tomography, and Fluoroscopy

The first type of x-ray, the one Jenny had, is called *radiography*. An x-ray image recorded on film, called a *radiograph*, is a permanent record of the image made by x-rays going through a part of the

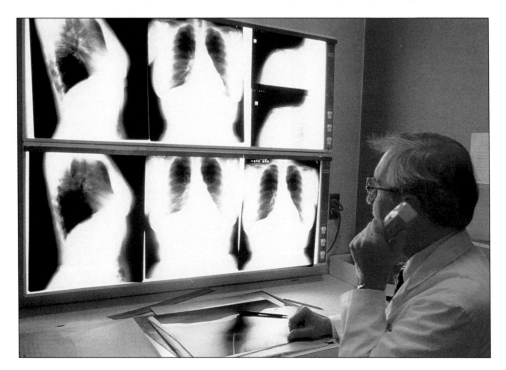

A doctor studies x-rays against a light box. Images like these, recorded on film, have been used by doctors for one hundred years. Recently, many new imaging techniques have been developed.

body and striking a film. Although we call it a "picture," it's really a record of shadows of the body parts, which vary in how dark they appear on the film by the amount of x-rays they absorb. Bone and other dense tissues absorb a lot of x-rays so the rays don't strike the film, making the dense tissue's image on the film appear lighter. Surrounding soft tissues allow more of the rays to pass through and strike the film so their images appear darker.

Doctors use radiographs to examine all the bones in the body. They can check that a broken bone is set properly and that it's healing the way it should, they can find stones in the gallbladder or kidney, and they can see symptoms of diseases such as cancer or tuberculosis. Radiographs are also what dentists use to examine teeth and find any cavities lurking inside.

A second use of x-rays is called *tomography*. Instead of looking at a body part straight on, as if you were seeing it in front of you, tomography uses x-rays to picture a "slice" of the body. It's as if you cut a slice from an orange, laid it flat, and took an x-ray of the slice. This process produces an image of what's happening inside a soft-tissue body part. Doctors find various form of tomography especially helpful in studying the chest, lungs, skull, and spine.

A third use of x-rays is called *fluoroscopy*. This type of x-ray allows doctors to study internal organs while they are in motion: the heart pumping or the digestive tract moving food along. A fluoroscope screen is covered with a chemical that gives off light when x-rays hit it. When the rays pass

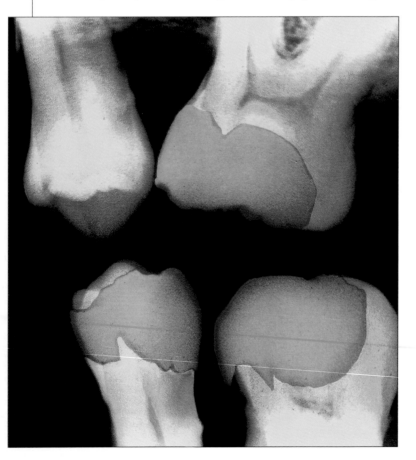

Dentists regularly use x-rays to find hidden problems with their patients' teeth. In this false-color image, the red areas are fillings and the green area in the tooth at bottom left is a decayed area waiting to be filled.

through a body and then hit the screen, an image of that body appears on the screen. It can be difficult to see the internal organs clearly on a fluoroscope screen because they appear rather hazy, so the patient is often given barium or some other radiopaque material (that is, it absorbs x-rays) to make the organ stand out more clearly.

Radiography, tomography, and fluoroscopy all have something in common. They all have as their foundation the work done by scientists a hundred years ago. Those men and women had no idea the mysterious rays they discovered and experimented with would one day allow doctors to peer into the farthest recesses of the human body to help rebuild structures and cure disease.

Exciting Discoveries

Today when we think of scientific research, we picture big laboratories full of microscopes and equipment loaded with dials and gauges, places where scientists expand our knowledge of the world. But one hundred years ago, that's not how laboratories looked. They were often tucked into an odd corner of a university or even in the attic, basement, or barn of a scientist's home. They were small; a lot of the equipment used today hadn't been invented yet. Despite these limitations, scientists in the 1800s had made many discoveries.

They knew quite a lot about electricity, for example, and were able to produce it in a laboratory. After trying for years to create a vacuum — a place where there is no air — they had

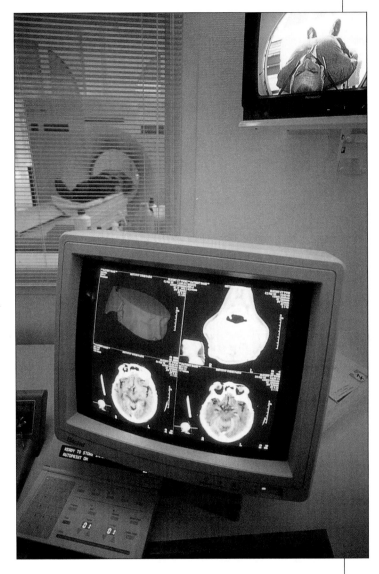

Tomography shows cross sections, or slices, of a body. The advanced machine shown here scans two sections of the spine at once. They are transformed by a computer into two- and three-dimensional images. The patient can be seen in the background and on the screen at the top of the picture.

learned to pump most of the air out of a glass tube to create at least a partial vacuum. That knowledge played a crucial role in the next big discovery.

Roentgen and the "Invisible Light"

One November afternoon in 1895, a professor of physics at the University of Würzburg in Germany was experimenting with a type of vacuum tube called a Crookes tube (named after the English physicist, William Crookes, who invented it). Crookes tubes were pear-shaped tubes, handblown from molten glass. Most of the air was sucked out, and two wires were inserted at the ends. The wires could be connected to a generator to carry electricity through the tube. Scientists had known for years that when electricity ran through a Crookes tube, a light glowed inside the vacuum at the other end, but they didn't know why.

Wilhelm Roentgen wanted to muffle this glow, so he built a black cardboard box around his Crookes tube. He pulled all the drapes in his lab to make it very dark and turned on the electrical generator. Just as he planned, no light showed through the black box, but across the room, his eye caught a glimmer of light. What was that?

Roentgen looked around his lab. On a table a few feet away from the Crookes tube were some objects he was going to use in a later experiment, including a sheet of paper fastened to a wooden frame. The paper was painted with chemicals that made it glow in the dark after a bright light shone on it, much like

Cartoon of Wilhelm Roentgen from around 1900. Artists were quick to find the humor in being able to see the skeleton through a person's clothes.

a toy that glows in the dark after a child holds it up to a light. Roentgen saw that the paper glowed as long as the electricity was on and running through his Crookes tube.

Some kind of ray must have been coming out of the Crookes tube. It was traveling right through the cardboard box without hurting it, speeding through the air, hitting the paper and making it glow. He had no idea what it was.

When scientists run into something unknown they often give it the name *x*. Since Roentgen couldn't identify the ray, he called it the *x-ray*, a name that has stuck.

Learning More About the Mysterious Ray

Roentgen was so excited by his discovery that he spent the next several weeks in his lab — he had his meals sent in and even had his bed moved in so he could work around the clock.

Thinking about this mysterious ray, Roentgen had another idea. Photographic film in those days was really a sheet of glass, called a plate, coated on one side with chemicals similar to those that are on a sheet of modern photographic paper. Working on a hunch, he put a photographic plate in front of his tube and turned on the electricity. The plate became foggy, as if he had ruined it by exposing it to too much light.

That gave him still another idea. He persuaded his wife, Anna, to put her hand on a photographic plate while he sent the mysterious x-ray through it. She had to be patient, standing absolutely still with her hand on the plate for many minutes. When Roentgen developed the plate, there was Anna's hand!

The bones looked like ghostly white shadows because the dense bone was harder for the rays to penetrate than soft flesh. The two rings she wore stopped the rays and were very clear in the picture. When Roentgen showed Anna the picture, she couldn't believe she was seeing her own skeleton.

Roentgen wrote about his discovery as ". . . a new kind of invisible light. It was clearly something new; something unrecorded."

AMAZING FACTS

At first, taking an x-ray was a slow process; the x-ray of Anna Roentgen's hand took half an hour. A few months later, x-rays were being done in five minutes. Today, they take only milliseconds.

Wilhelm Roentgen (1845–1923)

Wilhelm Roentgen was born in 1845 in Lennep, a small town on the Rhine River in the part of Germany called the Ruhr Valley, where many industries are located. He was the only child in his family; his father was a merchant. When he was three, the family moved to Apeldoorn, Holland.

Young Roentgen started his studies at the Utrecht Technical School, but he was expelled because his teachers blamed him for drawing an unflattering cartoon of a professor. Even though it was really another student who drew the cartoon, the incident kept him out of several colleges.

Finally, he passed an entrance examination for the Polytechnical School in Zurich, Switzerland. He graduated as a mechanical engineer in 1868, and in 1869, he received a doctorate from the University of Zurich. Four years later, he met and married his wife, Anna.

They spent the next seven years at the University of Strasbourg, where Roentgen investigated a number of different problems in the field of physics. He did research on determining specific heats, electrical discharges, radiation from the sun, improvements to the telephone, and the properties of crystals. His published work began to attract attention in the scientific community, and in 1879, while only thirty-four years old, he became professor of physics at the University of Giessen in Hesse. There, he did more research, leading to a discovery that he later considered as important as the x-ray. While investigating the "Rowland effect" (which demonstrated that a body in motion produces a magnetic field similar to the one created by an electric current in a conductor), he proved that when a material that doesn't readily conduct electricity is moved between two electrically charged condenser plates, the result is a magnetic effect. He called this the "Roentgen current."

In 1888, he became professor of physics and director of the new Physical Institute of the University of Würzburg. There, he did his most famous research and discovered the x-ray.

Roentgen was given many special honors for his discovery, including the first Nobel Prize in physics in 1901. He was also given the gold Rumford medal from the Royal Society in London, a medal from the Franklin Institute in Philadelphia, and another from Columbia University. One award he got from the German government carried with it the title of a nobleman but, although he accepted the award, Roentgen turned down the title.

Later, he moved to the University of Munich. In 1919, his wife died; he grew very sad and retired from the university the next year. He kept a small laboratory there and continued to do some research well into his seventies. Roentgen died in Munich in 1923; according to his wishes, his body was cremated along with all his papers and personal letters.

A cartoon from 1896, soon after Roentgen announced his discovery of x-rays.

THE NEW ROENTGEN PHOTOGRAPHY.

"Look pleasant, please."

Spreading the Word

After several more weeks of experimenting, Roentgen decided it was time for the world to know about his discovery. He wrote a paper titled "A New Kind of Ray," which was published by the Physical Medicine Society of Würzburg. In January 1896, he did the first public demonstration of his ray, x-raying the hand of one of his university colleagues in front of a group of fellow scientists. When the developed film was shown, the audience burst into applause.

Even newspapers picked up the story; front pages around the world were soon decorated with ghostly skeletons of people's hands or feet.

Some scientists, however, were skeptical of the discovery. One magazine, *Scientific American,* said in a January 1896 article that "the process will probably prove to be of scientific rather than of practical interest."

Some papers printed ridiculous stories about the newly discovered x-ray. One wrote that it was a threat to women because the rays could see through their clothes and offered x-ray proof underwear for sale! Another suggested that x-rays could be used to beam anatomy diagrams directly into students' brains, making learning easier.

However, other publications realized how important the x-ray would become. *The Nation,* another magazine, declared, "The application to surgery as an aid to diagnosis in cases of disease or fracture of the bones is apparent." After all, the writer went on, doctors previously had

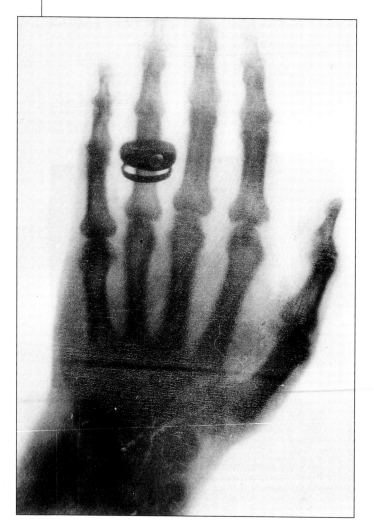

A print from one of Roentgen's early x-rays shows how the beams pass through skin much more easily than through bone and how they are absorbed by metals.

Early American x-ray apparatus from 1896. The man on the left is holding his hand against a photographic plate, while x-rays are produced from the electrical equipment on the right.

no way to see what was going on inside the body, and the x-ray would save patients the long, painful examinations they had had to undergo for a broken bone to be diagnosed.

Roentgen received many scientific honors, although, being a modest person, he turned down some of them. One of the most important he received was the Nobel Prize in physics in 1901. He gave the prize money to his university to use in scientific research. His discovery provided the foundation for further research that would change the world of medicine.

AMAZING FACTS

A writer submitted a poem to the American magazine *Photography* that read:
"I'm full of daze,
Shock and amaze
For nowadays
I hear they'll gaze
Thru' cloak and gown
— and even stays
These naughty, naughty
Roentgen rays."

Chapter 2
The Curies Find New Elements

Just a year after Roentgen discovered the x-ray, a French scientist, Henri Becquerel, was doing further experimenting with it, working with different chemicals to see if they would send out x-rays if the sun shone on them. He would wrap a photographic plate in black paper (so no light could get through), put a metal sheet on top of the wrapped plate, and dust it with different chemicals. He'd leave the whole contraption out in the sun, then develop the film to find out if the chemical had produced any x-rays to darken it. Only one metal, uranium, had worked.

Disgusted by a run of cloudy weather, Becquerel tossed a plate prepared with the wrappings and uranium into a drawer. A few days later, on some impulse, he developed the plate even though it had never been in the sun. Imagine his surprise when he found the plate darkened — without the sun. Some kind of rays must be coming from the uranium itself. Further experiments convinced him that the rays were not x-rays but a new property of the uranium atoms. Becquerel didn't know it, but he had discovered radioactivity, which scientists sometimes call radiation. However, he never investigated those mysterious rays any further.

Marie Curie Goes Beyond Becquerel

In the meantime, a young woman from Poland, Manya Sklodowska (who later changed her first name to Marie), had come to Paris to study at the famous Sorbonne University. She had quickly completed master's degrees in physics and mathematics and had married a young French scientist named Pierre Curie.

Now, she needed a subject for her doctoral thesis — a long, complicated research paper. Marie was fascinated by Becquerel's research and all the questions it had left unanswered. She decided to try to find some of those answers.

First, Curie had to find a way to measure the strength of the x-rays. Her husband had already invented a device called an *electrometer* that could measure the electric charge in the air. X-rays bleed off the charge on an object and their strength is measured by how fast the charge bleeds off. Marie could thus use the invention to measure the strength of radiation emitted by a substance.

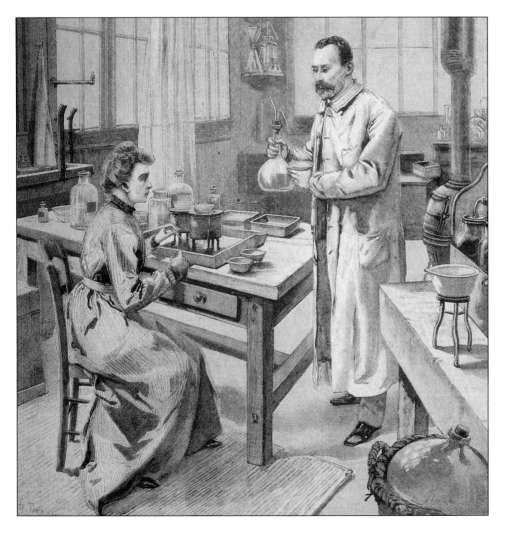

This French illustration of the time depicts Marie and Pierre Curie at work in their laboratory, looking for new radioactive elements. They began their search shortly after Becquerel's experiments with uranium in 1896, and by the end of 1898, they had detected two new radioactive elements, polonium and radium.

Marie Curie (1867–1934)

Marie Curie's intelligence and ambition led to a lot of "firsts": first woman in Europe to receive a doctorate degree, first woman to become a professor at the Sorbonne University in Paris, first woman elected to the Academy of Physicians in France, first woman to win a Nobel Prize. But she is best known as the first person (along with her husband, Pierre) to discover and isolate the element radium, a major source of radioactivity.

The story of how Madame Curie accomplished so many firsts starts in Warsaw, Poland, in 1867, when she was born Manya Sklodowska. A very bright child, she read fluently by age five and later loved to read technical books from her educated parents' library. She won a gold medal for her work in high school, but in Poland, women could not go on to the university. She needed to go to Paris for that, but the family couldn't afford to send her.

Marie and her older sister, Bronya, hatched a plan. Marie would work as a tutor and governess to send Bronya to medical school in Paris; when she finished, Marie would come live with her and take her turn at college.

The plan worked. Marie went to Paris in 1890. She was behind the other students, both in French and in science, but she studied day and night and passed her first exams at the top of her class. In 1894, she met Pierre Curie, a respected scientist and teacher in Paris; they married a year later and began the partnership that resulted in the discovery of radium.

For the Curies, 1903 was a big year. Marie was granted her doctorate and, in

Marie Curie at work in about 1905.

December, they were awarded the Nobel Prize in physics, jointly with Henri Becquerel, for their work on radium.

Just three years later, Pierre was crossing a busy Paris street on a rainy spring afternoon when he was run over by a horse carriage and killed instantly. His death was very hard for Marie and her two daughters, Irène, age eight and, Eve, just fourteen months.

Marie was asked to present the lectures Pierre had been giving at the Sorbonne; she was the first woman to lecture there. She also worked tirelessly to establish the Radium Institute in Paris and collected all of both her and Pierre's work and published it. In 1911, she was awarded a second Nobel Prize, this one for chemistry.

A few years later, World War I broke out. Realizing how valuable x-rays would be to injured soldiers, Marie Curie raised money and supplies to build a mobile x-ray vehicle. She taught herself to drive and she, Irène (then seventeen years old), and some other volunteers took the x-ray machine from hospital to hospital on the front lines. After the war, Marie continued to teach and raise money for research (including a trip to the United States in 1921 to receive the gift of a gram of radium) despite her failing health from radiation poisoning.

Blind from cataracts and plagued by joint problems and high fevers, Marie Curie died in a tuberculosis sanatorium in 1934, at the age of sixty-six. Her contributions to the science of medicine, through developing x-rays and radiation therapy, have saved many lives.

Irène, the Curies' oldest daughter, was also involved in radiation research. Their other daughter, Eve, wrote a biography of her famous mother.

An x-ray van used in World War I. Marie and Irène Curie drove vans like this between hospitals where wounded soldiers were being treated.

She tested many different minerals and metals; at first, the only one that gave out rays was uranium. It didn't take long for her to figure out that the strength of the rays depended on the amount of uranium in her samples. If there was uranium, no matter what it was mixed with, the rays were there. The more uranium, the stronger the rays.

Then, she found another substance that also gave off rays, although they were not as strong: thorium. She realized that the name she'd been using, uranium rays, wasn't accurate; obviously, a new name had to be coined. Calling on her imagination, she named the rays *radioactivity*.

The Hard Work of Research

At this point, Curie thought that only two elements, uranium and thorium, gave off the rays. Then, she made a discovery that surprised her: While testing an ore called pitchblende, she found it to be even more radioactive than either uranium or thorium. There must be something in pitchblende that sent out even more rays than those two elements. Could it be a new, unknown element? Pierre joined in her research. They decided to separate out all the known elements in pitchblende. Whatever was left had to be the new element.

The Austrian government offered them a ton of pitchblende. The research work was exhausting; it meant lugging around heavy vats of ore and buckets of water, stirring and pouring. It took four years, but by the end of their analysis, the Curies had found not just one new radioactive element, but two!

The New Elements: Amazing but Dangerous

The first new element, which the Curies named *polonium* after the country of Marie's birth, turned out to be a rather minor source of radiation. The second, however, which they called *radium*, is the most radioactive substance on earth.

AMAZING FACTS

When the Curies needed pitchblende for their experiments, the only place it was available was from a state-owned mine located in Joachimstal, Bohemia, now part of the Czech Republic. It was used to give Bohemian glass its beautiful clear green color but was considered worthless outside that use. The Austrian government offered the Curies a ton of pitchblende free, but they would have to pay the transportation costs. Since Marie had no income, they had to take the money from Pierre's low salary. Later, after the publication of their first results, they began to get some money from the Academy of Sciences. An anonymous donor also helped them.

Unfortunately, in those early days no one realized the dangers of radiation. Today, scientists protect themselves with radiation-proof gear whenever they work with radioactive substances. The Curies had none of that protection. They even used themselves as guinea pigs. Pierre once put a radioactive substance on his arm to see what would happen — it left him with a severe radiation burn that took a long time to heal. Marie often handled radioactive materials with her bare hands; she dismissed the burns she got as a minor annoyance. Both of them suffered from health problems, such as fatigue, aching joints, and blood disorders, that we know today are symptoms of radiation poisoning.

Protective clothing used in x-ray work in 1909. It had taken a few years for doctors and scientists to realize the dangers of x-rays, but then they began to take precautions such as wearing protective clothing.

But despite their ignorance of the dangers, scientists all over the world began experimenting with radium and radioactivity. One team was the Curie's daughter, Irène, and her husband, Frédéric Joliot, who worked on developing an artificial source of radioactivity.

The Curies were showered with honors including the Nobel Prize in physics in 1903; Marie did get her doctor's degree — the first woman in Europe to do so. Irène (who earned her own doctorate in physics doing research on polonium) and her husband shared another Nobel Prize in 1935.

The work done by Becquerel and the Curies laid the foundation for one of the specialized parts of the modern field of radiology: using radiation to treat diseases, especially cancer.

Irène Joliot-Curie (1897–1956) and Frédéric Joliot-Curie (1900–1958)

The oldest daughter of Marie and Pierre Curie, Irène Joliot-Curie, and her husband, Frédéric, were important researchers in their own right. Irène was born in Paris in 1897. She got her education at a cooperative school organized by her mother; the teachers included several important physicists. She graduated from the College Sevigne and entered graduate school at the Sorbonne in Paris. Her studies were interrupted by World War I, when she left school for several months to serve as an army nurse, helping her mother drive x-ray equipment to the wartime hospitals. After the war, she became a research assistant at the Radium Institute, which her mother

founded. In 1921, she started on her own research project dealing with alpha particles, atomic particles that consist of two protons and two neutrons; that research led to her doctoral degree.

Frédéric Joliot was born in Paris in 1900. He was interested in science from the time he was a child, so when it came time for college, he chose an engineering school in Paris and graduated with a degree in engineering. In 1925, he also became a research assistant at the Radium Institute where he met Irène Curie. Within a year they were married.

In 1931, the Joliot-Curies (the name they chose for themselves) began working together on a research project. Their work was the foundation that led to another scientist's discovery of the neutron, a part of the atomic structure.

While working with atomic byproducts, they accidently found they had created some radioactive substances that didn't exist in nature. Continuing their research, they created many new radioactive substances. In 1935, they shared the Nobel Prize in chemistry for their work.

A year later, Irène became a full professor at the Sorbonne; she also became director of the Radium Institute and continued her research on radioactivity. Frédéric went on to open a center of research in nuclear physics and chemistry. There, he proved that uranium atoms could be split and that this division could cause an explosion. After World War II started, he smuggled some of his research to England where it was used in the British effort to build an atomic bomb.

Both Frédéric and Irène were active in the French resistance against the Nazis during World War II; Frédéric joined the Communist Party in 1942, which caused some controversy later in his life. In 1944, they and their two children fled from Paris to Switzerland, where they lived until the war ended. After the war, Frédéric remained active in politics and served as president of the World Organization of the Partisans of Peace.

Irène died in 1956 of acute leukemia, probably from radiation poisoning. Frédéric took over as director of the Radium Institute and also took on her teaching duties at the Sorbonne. In 1958, two years after becoming ill with viral hepatitis, Joliot died of internal bleeding after an operation.

— Chapter 3 —
Early Radiology

It didn't take long after the discovery of the x-ray for doctors to begin using it on their patients. The first "radiologists" were either photographers or doctors who had some experience with photography as a hobby.

Early x-ray equipment was hard to acquire and not easy to use; many doctors relied on independent operators to do x-rays of their patients. Just a year after Roentgen presented his new ray to the public, people were advertising "Roentgen studios" that did "Roentgen photography." People were urged to make an appointment for an "x-ray sitting." Most of the studios did mainly medical x-rays, but some offered to x-ray other objects, such as jewelry, sculpture, metal castings, and even mummies.

There was no medical training required to do x-rays; in fact, there wasn't even any requirement for training in how to use the equipment. Many doctors learned how, and some operators who were not doctors took some medical training, but there were no standards or certification.

X-Rays Promoted as a Miracle

X-rays were the hit of the Crystal Palace Exhibition in London in 1896. A flyer handed to exhibition visitors urged them, "Before leaving the exhibition see the wondrous x-rays, the Greatest Scientific Discovery of the Age. See through a sheet of glass, through a block of wood, count the coins within your purse."

One x-ray studio in Chicago, Dr. Pratt's X-Ray and Electro-Therapeutical Laboratory, ran an advertisement calling itself the

STRAND-IDYLL Á LA RÖNTGEN

This cartoon from 1900 illustrates the obsession people had with the human skeleton now that they could see it for the first time as part of a living body.

"oldest x-ray laboratory" even though the x-ray itself was brand new! The ad said, "General Electrotherapeutical work of all kinds. Dr. Pratt's long experience enables him to guarantee:

- No injurious effects from the x-ray
- X-ray pictures, both snap shots and time exposures
- Cancer, lupus and other forms of tuberculosis, inflamed joints and numerous ailments successfully treated."

Medical Radiology Becomes a Specialty

The first clinical medical x-ray in the United States was done at Dartmouth College in New Hampshire on February 3, 1896. It was an x-ray of a fractured forearm. The same day, a doctor in Montreal, Canada, was the first to use the x-ray to locate a bullet in a patient's leg. Hospitals began using x-rays about the same time. The first Crookes tube for x-rays was set up in Massachusetts General Hospital in early 1896, and seven years later the Children's Hospital in Boston opened a "Department of Roentgenology."

Doctors quickly learned how to use the new tool more effectively. One of the ways they learned was to take x-rays of a patient, then, when the patient died, perform an autopsy and compare what was found to the x-ray. That way, doctors slowly learned how to apply the knowledge gained through an x-ray to treat real patients.

AMAZING FACTS

The first criminal case in America in which an x-ray was used as evidence happened in 1897. A man had been shot in the jaw with a .32 caliber bullet. Another bullet was lodged in the back of his head; the defense needed to know whether that one was a fragment of the first bullet or a different one. The man's head was x-rayed; the second bullet was not .32 caliber. There was a lot of arguing among the lawyers about whether or not an x-ray could be admitted as evidence, but the judge ruled that it could.

Francis Williams (1852–1936)

Sometimes called America's first radiologist, Francis Henry Williams was born in Boston in 1852. He graduated as an engineer from the Massachusetts Institute of Technology and then got a medical degree. His engineering background meant he understood much more about the technical part of radiology than most doctors did.

Williams was a doctor at Boston City Hospital, where he did his early studies on his patients. Working with other researchers, he helped design more powerful x-ray equipment that could take sharper radiographs using shorter exposure times. By 1896, x-ray exposures could be as short as a fifth of a second.

One of the areas Dr. Williams specialized in was fluoroscopy of the chest. In the late 1890s, he did a great deal of work on understanding the structures of the chest cavity. He gave lectures on and wrote detailed descriptions of the appearance of the normal heart and lungs on the fluoroscope screen. He was also one of the first doctors to use x-rays to diagnose pneumonia and to describe the appearance of the lungs as pneumonia disappeared and the lung tissue returned to normal. He also wrote descriptions of many other abnormalities in the chest including fractures, dislocations, bone diseases, and the appearance of foreign objects.

Dr. Williams demonstrated the value of x-rays very dramatically during a lecture he gave in 1896. He brought in one of his patients who had an enlarged heart. Before the lecture, Dr. Williams had drawn an outline of the man's heart by listening to its sounds on his chest. The outline was covered by a shirt. He put the man in front of a fluoroscope and traced the outline of his heart on the shirt. When the shirt was taken off, the outline on it matched the outline on his chest, showing that the x-ray was accurate. The doctors at the lecture were very impressed!

The next year, Williams wrote a paper summarizing his research. In it, he described how many different diseases and abnormalities look on an x-ray and some of the uses of x-rays in treating different diseases.

Dr. Williams also recognized the dangers of x-rays and wrote about how doctors should protect themselves and their patients. He

suggested that a sheet of metal with a hole cut in it be placed over the patient so the x-rays would enter the hole and be directed to only that part of the body being x-rayed. Unlike most radiologists of his time, he didn't suffer any serious radiation injuries.

In 1901, he wrote the first textbook on radiology, *The Roentgen Rays in Medicine and Surgery*. It was used by students for many years. Dr. Williams died in 1936.

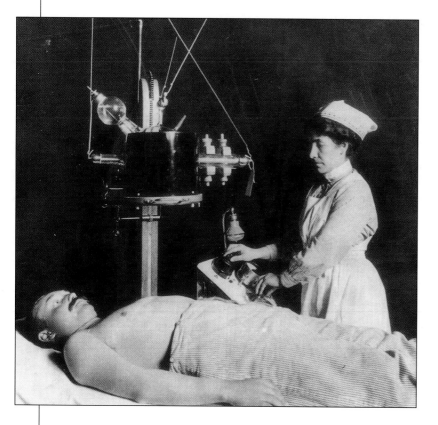

A nurse x-rays a wounded German soldier during World War I (1914–1918). Huge numbers of men were wounded in this war, and x-ray equipment proved valuable in helping treat many injuries.

Within a few years, some doctors were specializing in radiology, and others were seeing the value of sending their patients to someone who really knew how to do x-rays. The American Roentgen Society was formed in 1900; doctors who joined specialized in using x-rays for both diagnosis and treatment.

It wasn't long before doctors began to realize the dangers of x-rays as well as their potential to help. Doctors who did a lot of x-rays began to see changes in the skin on their hands, from peeling and shedding of the outer layer, to x-ray burns, and finally to cancers on exposed skin. Others noted their hair falling out and damage to their eyes.

In 1900, after some animal studies, a researcher, William Rollins, published safety guidelines for using x-rays in an article titled "X-Light Kills." He suggested that anyone using x-rays do three things:

- Wear glasses the rays can't penetrate.
- Shield the x-ray tube with lead (which x-rays can't penetrate).
- Aim the beam only at the part of the patient to be x-rayed and cover the rest of the person's body with lead shielding.

Not everyone listened at first, but slowly the word spread and getting an x-ray became safer.

As doctors did more and more x-rays, they learned a great deal about the process and how it could be made still safer and better. Their work through the years of the twentieth century has led to today's many types of medical x-rays.

Chapter 4
How X-Rays Are Produced

When you're outside on a sunny day, you're aware of radiation even if you don't know what it's called. The sunlight that warms your skin is a form of radiation. There are many other forms, but most of them you can't feel or see.

How are a lump of radium, an x-ray tube, a light bulb, a hot toaster, a radio transmission tower, and an electric power line related? They are all sources of electromagnetic radiation.

Electromagnetic radiation is energy traveling in waves; the waves are of different lengths, and the length gives each type its special properties. For example, x-rays and gamma rays penetrate the body and can damage its tissue, but light rays enter only the eyes, infrared rays warm every body part they touch, and radio waves pass by without our even being aware of them.

The electromagnetic waves that carry radio and television signals or cook food in a microwave are longer than the waves that create visible light. Other waves, such as the ultraviolet rays that tan your skin, are shorter than visible light waves. X-rays are also of this short-wave type. Short waves have more energy than long waves, and because of this they behave differently when they strike a target.

Creating X-Rays

To understand how the waves called x-rays work, you have to first understand what an electron is. Electrons are one part of matter,

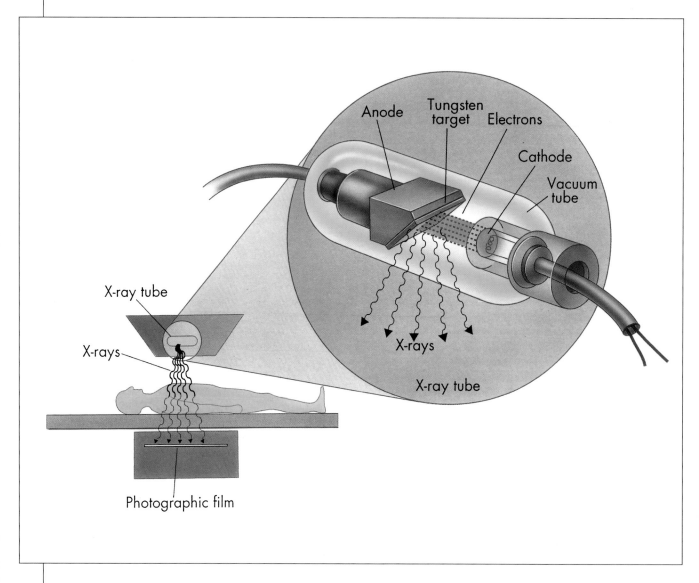

Anode Tungsten target Electrons

Cathode

Vacuum tube

X-rays

X-ray tube

X-ray tube

X-rays

Photographic film

X-rays are produced in a vacuum tube. When electrons are generated from a heated cathode, they stream toward an anode. On the face of the anode is a tungsten target. As the electrons strike this, they release x-rays.

the substance everything on earth is made from. You could consider the electron one of the building blocks of matter.

To produce x-rays you need three things: electrons, high-voltage electricity to make them move fast, and a target for them to hit. Electrons are not hard to produce. When something is heated to a high enough temperature, electrons "boil off." But producing electrons and using electricity to get them moving fast isn't enough to produce x-rays.

The electrons also have to hit something. When millions of electrons speeding through the air hit a metal target, they penetrate it. This releases x-rays. The faster the electrons are moving, the easier it is for them to penetrate the target. In an x-ray tube, some sort of metal is used as the target. The speeding electrons hit the metal, interact with the metal atoms, and produce the radiation we call x-rays.

The first x-ray tubes were the Crookes tubes Roentgen used. They weren't very effective because they didn't contain a complete vacuum, and there was no way to focus the electrons on a target. Tubes got more efficient as scientists bent them to target the electrons more closely and found better target metals such as platinum. However, x-rays cannot be focused or bent; they continue in the direction they were emitted in until they are absorbed.

W. D. Coolidge, here pictured with early x-ray equipment, invented an improved x-ray tube that replaced the Crookes tube that Roentgen had used.

Nearly twenty years after Roentgen's discovery, another researcher, W. D. Coolidge, made an even better tube. It had a true vacuum inside and was more stable and easier to control than the Crookes tube. Coolidge also found that using tungsten as the target produced more x-rays. Many, many improvements since those days have resulted in tubes that are smaller, much more efficient, and which produce more x-rays faster.

Using X-Rays

The tubes may have improved, but the basic method of x-raying a part of the body hasn't changed much through all the years of scientific discovery and improvement. The x-ray is still directed toward the body part being examined. The ray penetrates it, moving easily through soft tissue and being blocked by dense tissue such as bones or teeth.

After the x-ray film is developed, in much the same way photographic film is developed, it can be looked at on a view box where light shines through the film. The radiologist who reads the film, now called a radiograph, knows that it's like the negative of a photograph — the light and dark areas are reversed. The dense bones absorb more of the x-rays, so they show up lighter in the picture. Soft tissue lets more of the x-rays go through, so they show up darker. That's why the bones appear so ghostly on a radiograph.

A radiologist studies x-ray film, while on the light box in front of him are images produced with more recent imaging techniques. At top left are a series of computed tomography (CT) scans of a brain. Below, to the left of his arms, are a series of ultrasound scans. Plain x-ray film of a spine can also be seen.

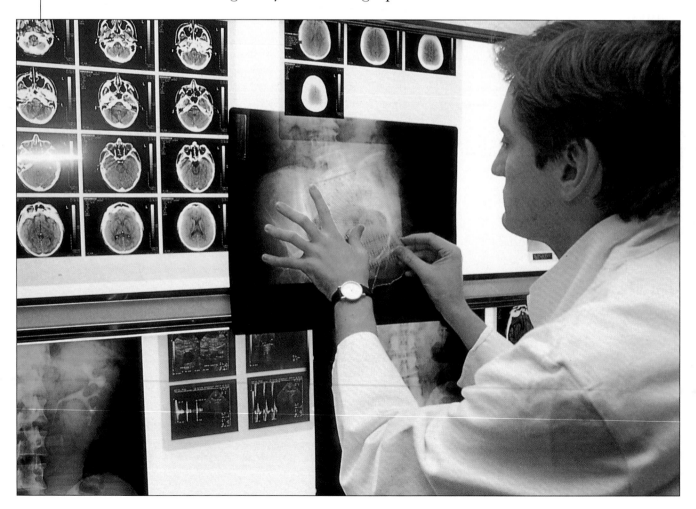

To see soft tissue more clearly, doctors can give the patient something called a *radiopaque* liquid, to drink. It absorbs the x-rays better than soft tissue alone can. A stomach filled with radiopaque liquid will show up much more clearly on a radiograph than an empty stomach. Often, technicians will also inflate the patient's stomach with gas and have the patient roll to coat the entire stomach with a radiopaque liquid such as barium.

Making Better Tools

Those speeding electrons bombarding a target metal have given medicine one of its basic tools, the x-ray. But in science, a basic tool is rarely enough. Scientists continually work to refine basic tools, making them yield more information, more precisely and more easily. X-rays are no exception.

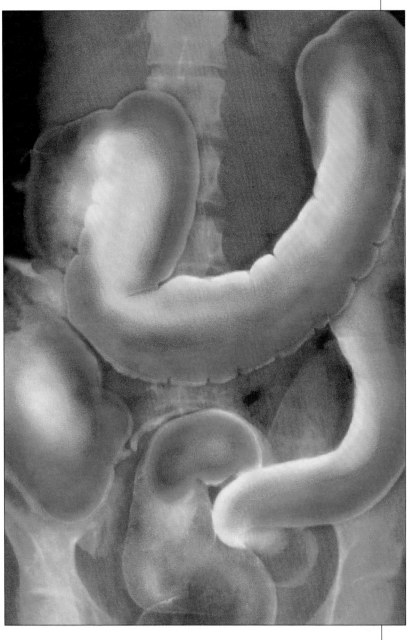

A colored x-ray image of a human abdomen shows the spine in the background and the large intestine, colored blue and green, at the front. The intestine has been infused with radiopaque barium sulfate.

Some of the new imaging technologies are more sophisticated and let doctors see much more than basic x-rays can. Many of these technologies use x-rays; some do not. But they are all grouped together under the term *medical imaging*. Imaging means making an image of part of the body. These new medical imaging devices are able to give doctors a wide variety of views inside the human body.

Chapter 5
Specialized Forms of Medical Imaging

New, more specialized forms of radiography, especially techniques that link the x-ray with the power of a computer, do more than Roentgen could ever have imagined.

Magnetic Resonance Imaging (MRI)

A scan of a human brain using Magnetic Resonance Imaging (MRI) shows a tumor (blue) occupying a large area of it. MRI scans are valuable in imaging soft tissue and do not use potentially harmful x-rays.

This form of radiology doesn't actually use traditional x-rays at all. Instead, an MRI uses a giant magnet along with a computer. An MRI machine looks like a narrow tunnel; the patient lies on a bed as it moves into the tunnel where it stops. The magnet generates a varying magnetic field, which cannot be seen or felt, around the patient. This field causes the hydrogen atoms in the body to line up. A radio signal is sent, knocking the hydrogen atoms off center; they wobble like tops. A computer measures the speed with which the atoms return to the center and uses that information to create an image of the inside of the body on a monitor similar to a television screen.

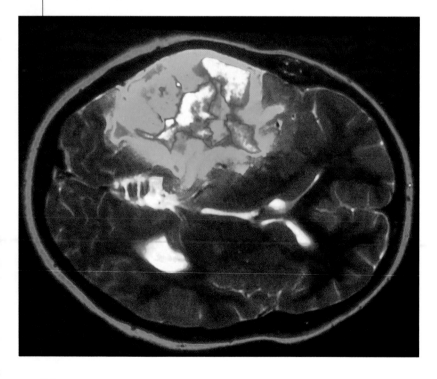

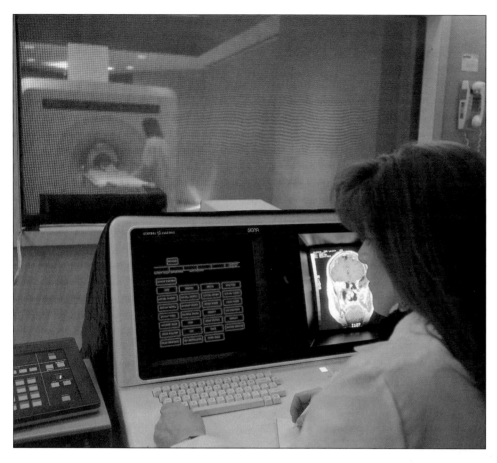

A radiographer conducts an MRI brain scan on a child. The patient can be seen in the background moving through the scanner's circular detector, and the scan appears on the video screen.

The body images can be created from front to back, from side to side, or in a cross section (like the orange slice we discussed previously). The MRI is especially good at making images of soft tissues, such as the brain and spinal cord, tendons, muscles, or arteries.

For example, if a person suddenly dropped to the floor with a seizure, doctors would need to know what was happening in his or her brain to cause the seizure. The MRI could be a lifesaver. A scan of the brain could show a tumor that no one had suspected was there. Such tumors can often be removed with brain surgery.

Computed Tomography (CT Scan)

Traditional x-rays teamed with a computer make CT scans valuable to doctors in diagnosing many different illnesses. A CT

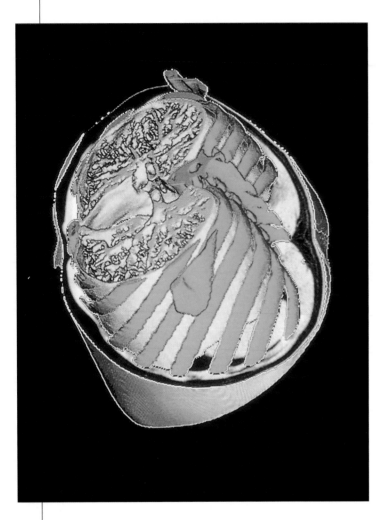

CT scans provide clear cross-sectional images of the body. X-ray absorption in body tissue is recorded and transformed into an image by a computer. This three-dimensional image of the chest cavity shows skin (white), bone (blue), and lungs (yellow).

scanner is a huge doughnut-shaped machine. The patient lies on a bed while the x-ray tube circles around his or her body, taking a series of "slice" views that are then transmitted to a computer. The computer can combine many thin slices into one picture, stacking them to create a three-dimensional (3-D) image. The image can be copied onto traditional x-ray film, or it can be stored in the computer for future use.

CT scanners, like the MRI, are very good at making images of soft tissue, such as the brain, but they are also excellent for making images of bones. Sometimes, when a bone has to be replaced with an artificial one, an engineer will use a 3-D picture from a CT scan to build the artificial bone. The engineer first uses the images from a CT scan to build a plastic model of the bone to be replaced. Then he or she uses the model to make an artificial bone that replaces the deformed or diseased one. A surgeon removes the bone and installs the implant.

Ultrasound

Ultrasound is another tool radiologists have that doesn't use x-rays. Ultrasound uses sound waves to create images of the inside of the body; it was developed from research the Defense Department did with underwater radar. To make an ultrasound image, a transceiver consisting of a transmitter and receiver is put somewhere on the body's surface. This device transmits a high-frequency sound wave through a person's skin. The receiver is passed simultaneously over the area; it picks up the sound waves and turns them into an image on a computer screen. An ultrasound exam doesn't use any radiation so it's safe, even for a pregnant woman whose fetus could be harmed by x-rays.

Ultrasound is also used for brain surgery and in checking the flow of blood in and out of the heart and in blood vessels around the body. But ultrasound is used most often to create an image of a fetus before birth. An ultrasound image created by passing the receiver over the mother's abdomen can tell a doctor the age of a developing fetus, how big its skull and abdomen are, whether or not its organs are normal, and even what sex it is.

Ultrasound can be a lifesaver for some babies. Problems such as heart defects can be detected before birth, and when the baby is born, specialists who can correct the problem can be standing by, ready to operate.

A pregnant woman and her family look at ultrasound scans of parts of the baby developing in her womb. Ultrasound uses high-frequency sound waves to produce images that can show if a baby is developing properly.

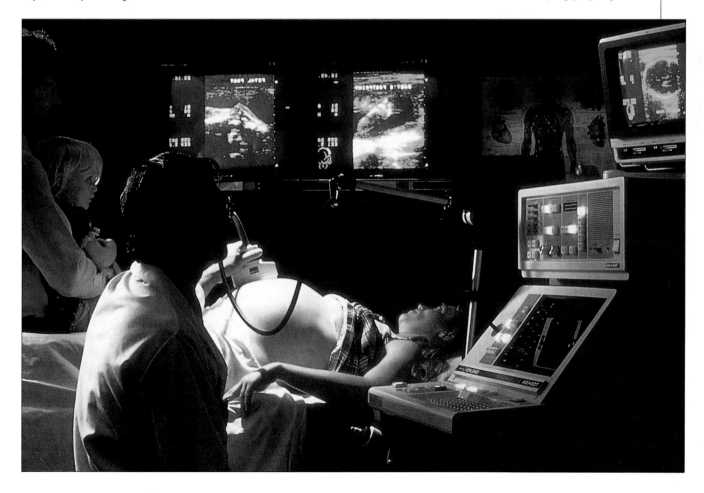

Positron Emission Tomography (PET)

A PET scan is a type of nuclear imaging. Nuclear imaging uses Marie Curie's discovery, radiation, and a camera called a *gamma camera* to capture an image of a beating heart, circulating blood, or the body's skeleton. Like a CT scanner, the two-ton machine is shaped like a big doughnut.

Before moving the patient into the scanner, the doctor injects a radioactive tracer (a dye or radioactive isotope) into him or her. Sometimes, the tracer may be swallowed or inhaled, depending on the part of the body being scanned. The bloodstream carries the radioactive tracer, which is harmless to the patient, throughout the body.

The patient is then rolled into the scanner and lies very still for fifteen or twenty minutes while the gamma camera sends an image to a computer screen. The PET scan is used most often to check a patient suffering from bone cancer or to see how efficiently the heart or lungs are working.

Mammography

A mammogram is an x-ray of a woman's breast to spot any cancerous tumors that may be growing in it. A woman having a mammogram stands in front of the x-ray machine with her chest against a screen. The x-ray technician takes x-rays from several angles to get radiographs of every part of the breast. Breast cancers show up as dark clouds in the lighter breast tissue.

Most medical x-rays are done only when there is a problem — a broken bone or some symptom such as pain in part of the body. But because breast cancer is such a serious disease for women and because it doesn't cause any symptoms until it's quite far advanced, doctors recommend that women have a mammogram checkup every two years after they turn forty and every year after age fifty. That way the radiologist can spot a breast cancer when it is still very small.

A small cancer can be cured by taking it out and treating the woman with radiation or anticancer drugs, but a large cancer is much harder to cure. That's why regular mammograms are so important to women; they reduce the death rate from breast cancer by finding cancers early while they are still curable.

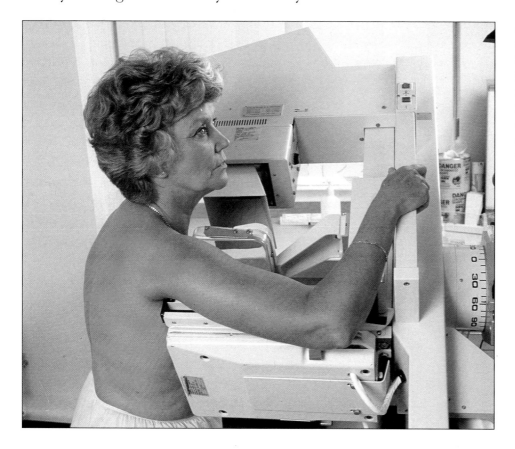

A radiographer positions a woman in front of x-ray film before taking a mammogram. These x-rays are performed regularly in order to detect breast cancers at an early stage while they can often be treated successfully.

Medical Imaging: A Valuable Tool

All these specialized forms of medical imaging have made an enormous difference in the lives of many people. They've prevented the need for surgery, made surgery more precise when it is necessary, and given doctors additional ways to help patients suffering from many different diseases.

But that's not all. Besides making medical images, radiology can actually treat disease. That's helped extend many people's lives, and improve the quality of the life they have left.

Rosalind S. Yalow

Until 1977, only one woman had ever won a Nobel Prize in medicine, and only five had won in any science category. On October 13, 1977, that changed. Rosalind S. Yalow received a phone call from Stockholm, Sweden, telling her that she had been awarded the Nobel Prize in medicine. She and her husband, Aaron, traveled to Stockholm to receive the prize and a handshake from the King of Sweden.

Born on the Lower East Side of New York in 1921, Yalow learned to read before entering kindergarten, and developed an interest in science, rare in girls in those days, while still in high school.

She entered Hunter College (now a part of the City University of New York) where she found her interest growing in the field of physics — again, a field that few woman entered. Yalow was the first woman to graduate from that college with a degree in physics — and she did it at the age of nineteen! She went on to become a teaching assistant and graduate student in engineering at the University of Illinois where she was the only woman in a class of over four hundred. She earned her doctorate in physics from the University of Illinois College of Engineering in 1945. Her research involved measuring radioactive substances.

Her work brought her to the attention of an important medical physicist, Dr. G. Failla. When Dr. Failla learned the Bronx Veteran's Administration Hospital was setting up a radioisotope service, he recommended Rosalind Yalow. She joined the hospital and established one of the first radioisotope laboratories in the country there. Radioisotopes are used to show where certain nutrients are concentrated in the body; they are tagged with radioactive atoms that can be traced.

She formed a research partnership with Solomon A. Benson, a physician specializing in internal medicine, and they used their combined knowledge of medicine and physics for twenty-two years. They developed a method, called RIA (radioimmunoassay) that uses radioactive materials to measure substances, such as hormones, that are present in very small amounts in blood plasma and other body tissue. Before Yalow's and Benson's work, some of those substances couldn't be measured at all; RIA can measure their presence in amounts as low as one-trillionth of a gram.

RIA is now used around the world to detect and measure hormones, drugs, the hepatitis virus, and levels of neurotransmitters (substances that conduct nerve impulses) in the blood. It is also used to detect cancer early and to screen children who are not growing normally to see if they have enough growth hormones in their bodies. Yalow and Benson's work was especially important in the field of diabetes research; they found that adult diabetics produce antibodies against insulin (the substance that helps break down sugar) that inactivate the insulin and make it less effective.

Unfortunately, Dr. Benson died before the Nobel Prize was awarded or he and Yalow would have shared it. When Dr. Yalow gave her Nobel acceptance speech, she spoke about the low numbers of women working in the sciences at that time. She said, "The world cannot afford the loss of the talents of half of its people if we are to solve the many problems which beset us. While we still live, let us join hands, hearts, and minds to work together for their solution so that your world will be better than ours and the world of your children even better."

Rosalind Yalow has also been awarded many other important prizes including the Scientific Achievement Award of the American Medical Association.

Rosalind Yalow celebrates with colleagues after hearing she is to be awarded the 1977 Nobel Prize in medicine.

—— Chapter 6 ——
Radiation Therapy

There are two basic ways radiology can be used in treating a variety of diseases. One of these is called angiography, the other is radiation therapy.

Clearing Clogs in the Bloodstream

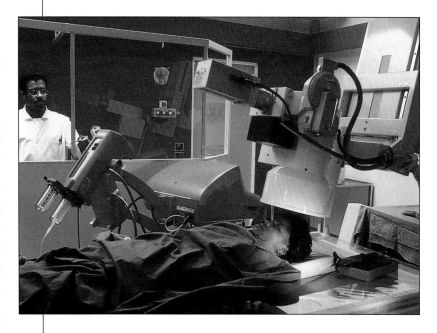

A patient undergoes an angiography examination of the arteries to the brain. Before this, radiopaque dye has to be injected into the bloodstream. This enables doctors to analyze the patient's blood circulation.

Surgery is hard on a patient. Even though it may be necessary to save a life, it's painful, it takes a long time to recover from, and it's expensive. Anytime something other than surgery can be used, it's better for the patient. Radiology is making it possible for doctors to do some things that used to require surgery, without it.

Probably the best example is opening clogged arteries in the heart. When the big blood vessels that carry oxygen-rich blood into the heart become blocked with a hard substance called plaque, the blood vessels get narrower, much like a water pipe choked with minerals that have built up inside. When the heart doesn't get enough blood, part of it dies; that's called a heart attack.

One solution to this problem is open heart surgery. The blocked arteries can be taken out and replaced with open ones, usually from the patient's leg or from arteries rerouted in the chest. But open heart surgery is difficult and has a certain degree of risk. Clearing the arteries without surgery, when it can be done, is preferable. Radiology is helping to do that.

First, radiology, in a form called *angiography*, can help in locating the block in the blood vessels. Radiopaque dye can be injected into the patient's bloodstream. The dye circulates through the blood vessels as the doctors watch using a fluoroscope (the type of x-ray that creates an image of a part of the body in motion) until they see the blockage.

Angioplasty: Surgery Without a Knife

Once they've found the blockage, they have several ways to open it, using a fluoroscope to guide them. In one method, called *angioplasty*, the doctor puts a hollow tube called a catheter into the patient's artery. Watching on the fluoroscope screen, the doctor guides the catheter through the arteries until it comes to the blockage. Then, he or she puts a small balloon through the catheter and into the blockage. The balloon is inflated; it squeezes the plaque back against the walls of the blood vessel, opening a bigger channel for blood to flow through. Sometimes the vessel is held open with a cylindrical metal case called a stint.

Instead of a balloon, doctors can also use a small rotating drill to shave away the blockage and sometimes a laser to vaporize it. Whatever method they use, the fluoroscope allows the doctors to see what they are doing. The same procedures are also used to unblock clogged arteries in the leg.

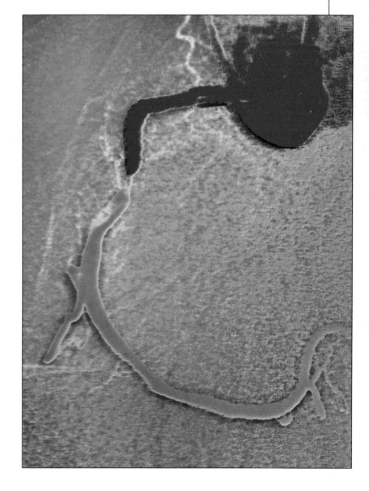

A colored angiogram taken during an operation to treat a narrowing of an artery in the heart. The narrowing can be seen (upper center left) and just below it is a blood clot. At top center of picture, a catheter with a cylindrical balloon has been inserted into the artery. As it inflates, the balloon opens the narrow blood vessel.

AMAZING FACTS

When radiation was first discovered, some people thought it was a miracle substance able to solve many problems.

• In 1929, a British magazine advertised a girdle lined with radioactive material as a cure for rheumatism. Another company offered electric blankets filled with uranium, saying they combined the advantages of heat and radioactivity. Radioactive material was added to hair tonic, chocolate bars, tooth paste and hearing aids during the 1920s and 1930s.

• A miniature soda fountain filled with a radioactive liquid was supposed to provide a "health drink" if taken every morning. One doctor called his version of the drink "Liquid Sunshine."

• Some scientists thought crop yields and the taste of food would be improved if radium was added to the soil. One farmer said radium should be put in chicken feed so the chickens would lay hard-boiled eggs!

Fluoroscope Guides Surgeons

The fluoroscope can help doctors open blood vessels; it can also do the opposite — help to stop blood from flowing through them. Cancer tumors can't grow if they don't have a blood supply; radiology allows doctors to locate tumors and find the blood vessels that supply them. Using the fluoroscope as a guide, a doctor can seal off the blood vessels that supply a tumor; it will then shrivel and die. Also, if a blood vessel bursts somewhere in the body, especially in the brain, doctors may use a similar technique to seal it off.

Patients can even benefit from treatments made possible by radiology before they are born. Doctors can correct some problems in a fetus before birth, using a type of fluoroscopy to guide them. For example, blockages in a fetus's brain or urinary system have been opened using special fluoroscopy to locate the blocks and guide the instruments.

Shattering Kidney Stones

Some people's kidneys tend to form small, hard stones that can get stuck in the ureters (the tubes that carry urine from the kidneys to the bladder) or in the urethra (the tube that carries urine from the bladder to the outside of the body) and cause a great deal of pain and damage to the tubes. Doctors used to have to do surgery to remove them.

But by using x-rays to pinpoint the exact location of the stone and a technique called *lithotripsy*, stones can be treated without surgery. The patient is lowered into a deep tank of water that covers the body, except for the head. Doctors use an x-ray to locate the stone, then they send an ultrasonic shock wave aimed at the stone rippling through the water. The wave enters the patient (who is under anesthetic) and shatters the stone into tiny grains of sand. The doctors watch on the x-ray to make sure all the stone has disintegrated. The patient feels a little sore

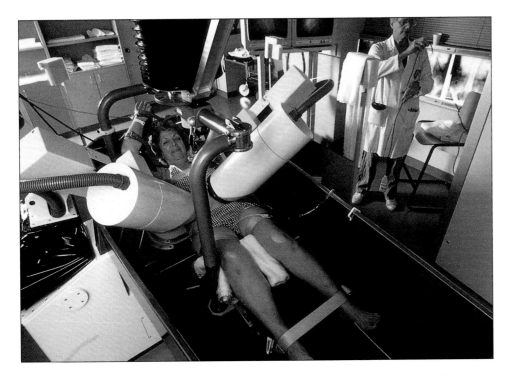

Lithotripsy uses ultrasound waves to break kidney stones into small fragments that can be passed out of the body in urine. The two cylindrical devices focus the sound waves into the kidneys. Before lithotripsy was developed, surgery was the only treatment available.

afterwards — rather as if he or she had been slugged in the back — but it's nothing compared to the pain of traditional surgery.

Radiation Therapy

As Marie Curie stirred her vats of water and pitchblende to try to find the unknown element that was sending out mysterious rays, she could never have guessed that someday her discovery would play a major role in curing people of cancer.

Cancer isn't just one disease. It's a whole group of diseases in which some cells in the body "go wild," multiplying and spreading uncontrollably. It can happen in just about any part of the body, even in several parts at once. The cells develop into clumps called tumors.

There are some tumors that are not cancer; we call them benign or nonmalignant. This kind of tumor will keep growing (they can become very large), but they don't spread to other parts of the body. Malignant tumors, or cancers, do spread. Cancer can invade nearby organs or create new tumors in a different part of the body. This process is called *metastasis*; it has very serious, often fatal results. Doctors have been doing surgery to remove cancerous tumors, with varying rates of success, for over one hundred years. But now they have a new weapon in fighting this terrible disease: radiation.

Radiation in Treating Cancer

Radiation therapy, sometimes called radiotherapy, is a specialized form of radiology that uses either x-rays or the rays produced by radioactive material (depending on the type of cancer) to destroy cancer cells. Sometimes it's used instead of surgery; sometimes it's used in addition to surgery, either before or after.

Radiation damages human tissue. That was obvious even back in the days of the Curies when doctors began to see the effects of radiation on people who did x-rays. The trick to using radiation therapy is to target the radiation just to the malignant cells so it will destroy them without harming the surrounding normal cells. Radiation therapy equipment allows the doctors and technicians to focus the rays closely to put them right where they are needed.

Radiation therapy used instead of surgery can shrink a tumor. Some tumors grow in a location where they can't be removed without doing extensive damage to important organs around them. That's often true with brain tumors. Radiation can shrink those tumors; sometimes they get smaller, sometimes they totally disappear. Often a tumor that can't be removed because of its size can be removed once it shrinks.

When a surgeon removes a malignant tumor, cancer cells can be left behind. They can begin to grow again in the same place, or they can migrate to a different part of the body and grow into a new tumor. There are two ways to fight these left-behind cancer cells.

One is with powerful drugs that kill the cancer cells but not normal cells — a treatment called *chemotherapy*. The other is with radiation therapy — using x-rays or radioactivity to kill the cells left behind. Some patients have chemotherapy, some have radiation therapy, and some have both.

The radiation therapy machine that's used most often is called a *linear accelerator*. The patient lies very still on a table; the radiologist positions the accelerator's head so the radiation is beamed directly at the cancer. Usually a patient gets radiation for just a few minutes each day for several weeks. The treatment isn't painful, although patients may feel somewhat sick afterwards or have red skin as if they had a mild sunburn. In some cases, radioactive material is put directly into the tumor and left in place; that treatment only works on certain kinds of tumors.

Doctors are experimenting with new drugs that are absorbed only by cancer cells. The drugs attract the circulating radioactive tracers into the cancer cells but not into normal

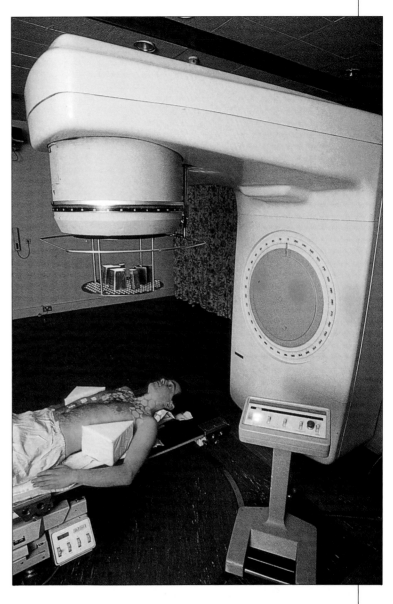

A patient undergoes radiation therapy for cancer. The radiation is directed to the neck and upper chest, and the areas to be treated appear as illuminated circles on the man's body.

cells that haven't absorbed them. They hope these drugs will focus the radiation even more closely and make radiation therapy less damaging to tissue surrounding the tumor. It's possible that someday radiation therapy may be so effective that cancer surgery will be very rare.

Cancer and other diseases have been among humankind's most devastating enemies. Some doctors have referred to fighting these diseases as a "war." Radiation therapy has given us one of our most powerful weapons in fighting that war.

Juan A. del Regato

Juan del Regato was one of the first doctors to specialize in treating cancer with radiology. Born in Camaguey, Cuba, in 1909, del Regato studied medicine at the University of Havana. While an intern, he was offered the job of radiological technician; although he didn't know anything about radiology, he learned on the job. In the early 1930s, radiation therapy for breast cancer was controversial; based on his experiences, del Regato wrote a paper on the practice. Thus, he began a life-long interest in radiation therapy for cancer — radiological oncology.

When political disturbances closed the medical school in Havana, del Regato finished his studies at the University of Paris. His thesis for his M.D. degree was on radiological treatment of patients with inoperable cancer of the jaw. After getting his M.D., Juan del Regato went on to study for a diploma in radiophysiology and radiotherapy. He was an assistant at the Radium Institute in Paris, where he helped care for patients and worked with them after their treatment. He also developed a device that attached to the radiology machine to shine a beam of light along with the rays to aid the radiologist. Later, General Electric used the lighting device on their radiology machines.

In 1938, del Regato came to the United States and joined a radiological practice in Washington, D.C., where he worked with radiation treatment for women with cervical cancer. There, he met his wife, Inez, a registered nurse. Later, he did research at the National Cancer Institute and served as director of radiotherapy at several hospitals in the United States.

While he was at the Ellis Fischel State Cancer Hospital in Columbia, Missouri, he and another doctor wrote a book on radiological treatment of cancer for other doctors and medical students. He also worked in clinical trials for radiation treatment for cancer of the prostate (a gland which affects urination in men). In 1949, he became the director of the Penrose Cancer Hospital in Colorado Springs, where he remained for twenty-five years. After retirement, he moved to Florida but soon returned to teaching at the University of South Florida, where he lectured three times a week even at an advanced age.

Dr. del Regato received honorary doctorates from three different universities, and was given many awards including the Scientific Achievement Award of the American Medical Association in 1993. That same year, he published a book of biographies of famous people in the radiology field called *Radiological Oncologists: the Unfolding of a Medical Specialty*. The book includes biographies of famous doctors and researchers in the field of radiological oncology (cancer treatment) from the 1850s to the present.

— Chapter 7 —
X-Rays in Industry

X-rays have been of so much benefit in the world of medicine that people sometimes forget that they are also valuable in other areas, especially in the world of manufacturing. Industries of all kinds depend on x-rays to improve the quality of their products. Without x-rays, it would be much harder to be sure that metal parts don't have any cracks or that containers of food or other products are really full to the brim.

X-Rays for Safety

When you are flying in an airplane or driving across a bridge, you want to be positive that the metal it's made from is solid and

A part of a helicopter engine is examined using a CT scanner. This allows the inside of the component to be seen in cross section on the screen in the foreground. Quality control testing like this finds structural defects in metal castings.

doesn't have any minute cracks or structural flaws. X-rays can find those flaws before they cause a tragic accident. An x-ray can penetrate a metal casting, for example, and make a radiograph that shows any holes, cracks, or other flaws. This process is called nondestructive testing because the material being tested isn't harmed. It's probably the most common industrial use of x-rays.

Airlines have benefitted in several ways from the safety x-rays offer. Besides nondestructive testing of airplane parts, x-rays are used extensively at airports to check baggage and passengers' carry-on bags for weapons.

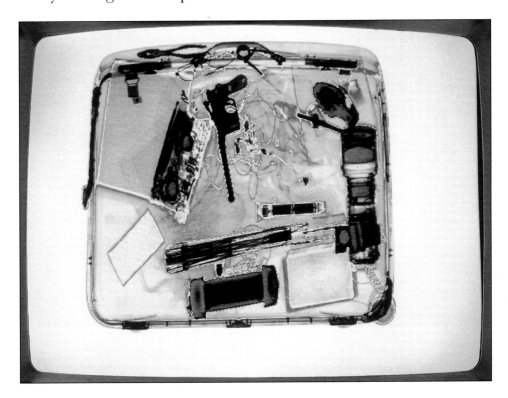

A modern airport x-ray scanner using color coding reveals the contents of a suitcase, including a block of Semtex plastic explosive (yellow, bottom left), a pistol, a hand grenade, and a telephoto lens.

Industrial Quality Control

In some manufacturing processes, x-rays are used to measure certain qualities in the product and to sense when they are not meeting required standards. If the x-ray sees that something isn't right, it can send a signal to a computer that will adjust the manufacturing process to correct the error. This kind of x-ray/computer combination is widely used in manufacturing metals, paper, cement, film, plastic, and rubber.

X-rays are also used to identify what substances are made from. Different elements give off different secondary rays when they are bombarded by x-rays. Measuring the wavelengths of these rays can tell a material engineer what elements the material is made from. The process is called *x-ray emission spectrometry*. A related process, called *x-ray diffraction*, allows researchers to identify crystal structures and the chemical compounds in the material.

A scientist uses x-ray diffraction equipment (in the background) and a computer to find the crystal structure of a protein. X-rays hit the crystal and spread out, hitting a detector plate. The position and intensity of the rays are analyzed and presented on the computer monitor.

In some manufacturing processes, the thickness of what is being made is critical — sheets of steel, for example, that vary in thickness would be useless. In a process called x-ray gaging, x-rays measure the thickness of sheets of metal, plastic, glass, paper, rubber, and aluminum foil as they are being made. If the gaging shows the products are not coming out of the manufacturing process at a uniform thickness, the manufacturer can then make the necessary adjustments to the process.

A different kind of x-ray process senses whether or not containers are full. Underfilling isn't a problem if the containers are glass, but when they're made from something opaque, like aluminum soda cans, it's hard to know if the machine is filling the containers to the right level without opening each one. This kind of x-ray device checks the level of each container and alerts the manufacturer if there is a short fill. The process is used for cereal boxes, milk cartons, drugs, motor oil, and even perfume.

Uncovering Fake Paintings

Radiography has been used in the art world to determine whether paintings are real or copies. X-rays of paintings can also be used in several other ways. They can determine what kind of pigments are in various paints, giving a clue as to how old the

Radiography was used to examine this seventeenth-century painting by Anthony van Dyck (left). It was irradiated, and gradually chemicals in different layers of the picture were revealed. After four days, areas of phosphorous, a component of charcoal, could be seen. This revealed a charcoal self-portrait of van Dyck (upside down, right), drawn on the canvas before he painted over it.

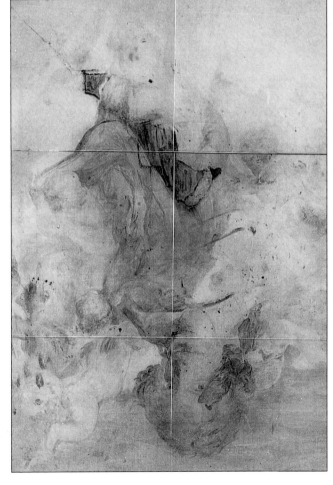

painting is. They can find an artist's signature hidden under layers of paint and if another painting lies underneath the one that shows. They can also discover places where repairs or alterations have been made to a painting.

In one case, a German art dealer in the 1930s was selling paintings he claimed were by the famous Dutch artist, Vincent van Gogh. He had sold thirty of these paintings to art collectors and dealers. Radiographs of the paintings showed that the underlying brush strokes were quite different from the type van Gogh used. The dealer was convicted of fraud and sent to prison for a year.

X-Rays Help Farmers Feed the World

X-rays have also been used in research labs where new strains of vegetables and fruits are bred. All the characteristics of plants, just as in animals, are carried in their genes. They are the blueprint a plant follows as it grows. Genes dictate whether a tree will produce red or green apples, for example, or whether corn stalks will have large or small ears of corn. To produce a plant that resists certain pests or diseases or produces a larger crop, scientists called geneticists manipulate these genes.

Let's assume that some scientists wants to produce a corn plant that will have larger ears of corn. They need to find plants that have the genes for big ears and breed them. But finding the correct genes can take a long time if you have to wait for them to happen naturally. Scientists have found a way to speed up the process. They expose plants to x-rays, which causes their genes to change, or mutate. Most mutations are not beneficial and are discarded. But a few mutations are of benefit to the plant. Scientists further breed the plants with these beneficial genes (such as one for large ears in corn) to make them better producers.

Who would think that objects as different as a carton of milk, an ear of corn, and an airplane engine would all benefit from x-rays? Roentgen would surely be impressed by the many uses his "invisible light" has been put to!

—— Chapter 8 ——
Radiology in the Future

In just one hundred years, the field of radiology has exploded from Roentgen's mysterious light and Marie Curie's new elements to highly sophisticated imaging equipment that has probed every area of the human body. Radiation-producing devices have helped to cure cancer, one of our greatest killers. If so much has happened in just a hundred years, what will happen in the future?

Surely, progress in radiology will continue at just as great a pace. Ever more sophisticated machines for diagnosis and treatment will be developed, and medical imaging and radiation therapy will become more effective, while becoming safer than ever.

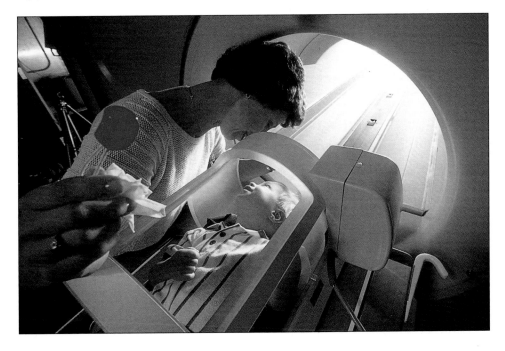

Watched by his mother, a young child is about to have an MRI scan. The scan is needed to investigate a heart defect and to plan corrective surgery. Modern imaging like this will do him no harm, and a computer will create helpful three-dimensional views of his heart from the scan data.

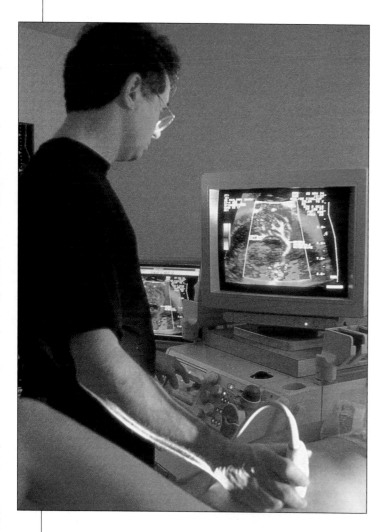

Ultrasound equipment can now be linked to a color video screen to provide high-definition images. Here, blood flow (yellow) is visible inside a fetus's head.

The Computer Link

One of the most exciting areas in radiology in the future is the continuing linkage, or interaction, of radiology machines and computers. Computers and radiology devices together will be used in more ways to increase doctors' ability to visualize the human body and to manipulate images to give them more information. Computers will help provide three-dimensional, sharply defined images, especially of the brain, but also of other body structures.

Magnetic Resonance Imaging will play a even larger role in diagnosis in the future. Radio waves coming back from a body within the magnetic field generated by the MRI will allow doctors to actually chemically analyze body tissues and permit them to interpret their chemical and electromagnetic functions.

Storing and Retrieving X-Ray Information

One major problem in radiology is how to store all the records the new imaging devices generate. It's one thing today to have file drawers full of x-rays and be able to find the one you need quickly, but imagine the problem when there are literally hundreds of views of each patient and thousands of patients around the country. Old-fashioned methods of storing information on x-ray films in file drawers won't work — the sheer number of films would overwhelm the system.

The computer/x-ray link will help in solving that problem. Digital storage systems — using numbers to describe the x-ray pictures and results — already exist and will be perfected in the future. In these systems, the image from a radiology device such as an MRI or a computed tomography scan is converted — or digitized — into information bits a computer can read. Then, they will be stored in the computer where they can be called up and reconverted into images when needed. That process avoids having to store actual x-ray films. It's like storing information on the hard drive in your computer instead of making hard copy and keeping it in a filing cabinet.

Besides eliminating the need to store all those films, that system will give instant access to the images to doctors all around the country. A doctor in Houston who is consulting on a case in Detroit will be able to call up the patient's x-ray results on his or her computer and not have to wait for the hospital in Detroit to mail the films.

Another method that will make information storage more efficient will be the use of voice-to-computer systems. Today, a

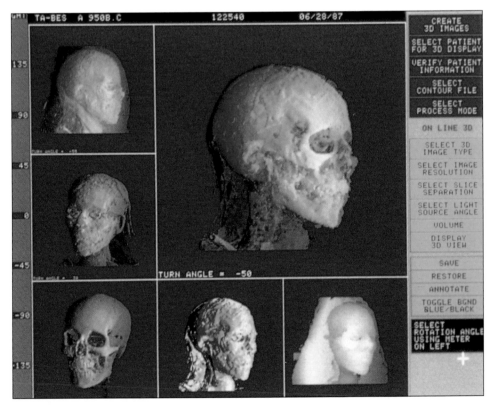

AMAZING FACTS

Before radiography, scientists interested in the mummies from ancient Egypt couldn't find out what was inside the wrappings without opening them, destroying the mummy. The first radiograph of a mummy was done in 1896. One researcher at the Vienna Museum got a big surprise: he x-rayed one of the museum's mummies and found it was a bird, not a human being! Radiographs have been used to find metal coins, statues and amulets wrapped right into a mummy without opening it. X-rays of mummies have also helped archaeologists determine what kinds of diseases the Egyptians suffered from. We know from these x-rays that broken bones and arthritis were common in ancient Egypt.

Modern radiography and tomography can tell us about people who lived thousands of years ago. These three-dimensional images of the head of a female Egyptian mummy were compiled from CT data. The examination was done to establish the medical condition of the woman when she died.

radiologist reads a film and dictates the results into a tape recorder. Someone transcribes the tape into a report that's sent to a referring physician. With a voice-to-computer system, the radiologist will be able to talk into a recorder that digitizes his or her voice and stores it, along with the image, in a computer. When it's called up later, the image and the report will be all together, easily accessible by other doctors.

Ultrasound Body Scans and Treating Tumors

Ultrasound images will become clearer and easier to interpret in the future. It's possible that doctors will carry a small ultrasound device as they now carry a stethoscope and pass it over a patient's body as part of a general assessment of the patient's condition. Gall stones or other abnormalities could show up immediately.

Radiology will be used to find the exact location of cancer tumors so doctors can destroy them with laser beams or microwaves. Radiology devices will keep track of progress as the tumor is destroyed.

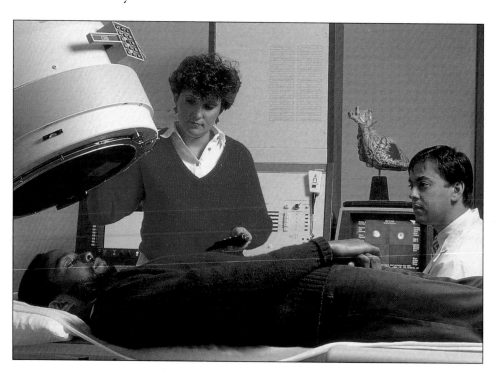

A gamma camera scans a patient's neck and upper chest. Gamma scans map the distribution of radioactivity emitted from a radioactive tracer in the patient's body. On the screen are colored tracer images made by the camera.

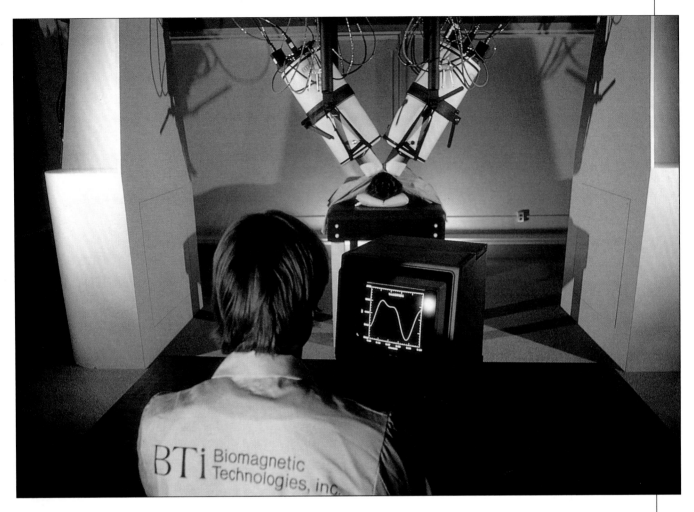

One promising field of research is using tiny devices called *superconductive quantum interference devices* (SQUIDs) that measure tiny biomagnetic fields. The human body produces some electrical energy that flows through the nervous system. SQUIDs are being used to make images of that flow; they might be useful in controlling epilepsy and other brain disorders.

New methods of imaging, new ways of storing information, new ways of sharing it with doctors all over the world — indeed, we have come a long way since Anna Roentgen held her hand on a photographic plate while her husband sent his newly discovered rays through it. With the dedication of thousands of research scientists all over the world, the next one hundred years will bring even more new ways to save lives and improve their quality.

This brain scan is using newly developed technology. Highly sensitive magnetic field detectors known as SQUIDs record data of nerve cell activity from up to forty sites around the brain.

Timeline

1895 — Wilhelm Roentgen discovers the x-ray.

1896 — Henri Becquerel discovers radioactivity. First public demonstration of the x-ray. First medical x-ray done in the United States.

1897 — Marie Curie begins researching radioactivity.

1900 — American Roentgen Society formed for doctors specializing in radiology. First warnings about the dangers of x-rays.

1902 — Marie and Pierre Curie isolate radium.

1916 — Coolidge x-ray tube is patented.

1930s — Research in imaging planes of the body done in France, Germany, and the U.S., laying the foundation for modern tomography.

1934 — Irène and Frédéric Joliot-Curie discover radioactivity can be artificially produced.

1947 — First medical use of ultrasound, after underwater radar was developed during the Second World War.

1972 — The first two-dimensional image created in England, leading to computed tomography and the CT scan. It couldn't have been developed much earlier because the system needs a powerful modern computer to work.

1979 — Balloon first used to open closed arteries in the heart.

1980 — First MRI of the human brain.

1980s — New ways to remove plaque blocking blood vessels are developed such as shaving it away and vaporizing it with a laser. In these methods, the doctor is guided by fluoroscopy. MRI becomes method of choice to image central nervous system. MRI angiograms (scans of blood vessels) are developed in which flowing blood shows up as brighter than surrounding tissue. Becomes best method to image blood vessels.

1990s — Ongoing development of digitized storage and retrieval systems to electronically store information from radiology devices.

Further Reading

Asimov, Isaac. *Quasars, Pulsars and Black Holes.* Milwaukee, WI: Gareth Stevens, 1988.

Fradin, Dennis. *Radiation.* Chicago: Children's Press, 1987.

Gherman, Beverly. *The Mysterious Rays of Dr. Roentgen.* New York: Macmillan, 1994.

Haber, Louis. *Women Pioneers of Science.* New York: Harcourt Brace Jovanovich, 1979.

McGowen, Tom. *Radioactivity: From the Curies to the Atomic Age.* New York: Franklin Watts, 1986.

Moche, Dinah. *Radiation: Benefits/Dangers.* New York: Franklin Watts, 1979.

Parker, Steve. *Marie Curie and Radium.* New York: HarperCollins, 1992.

Pflam, Rosalynd. *Marie Curie and Her Daughter Irène.* Minneapolis, MN: Lerner Publications, 1993.

Simon, Seymour. *Hidden Worlds: Pictures of the Invisible.* New York: Morrow, 1983.

Steinke, Ann. *Marie Curie and the Discovery of Radiation.* Chicago: Children's Press, 1987.

Veglahn, Nancy. *The Mysterious Rays: Marie Curie's World.* New York: Coward, McCann & Geoghegan, 1977.

Glossary

Chemotherapy: Treating cancer and other diseases with drugs or other chemicals.

Electrode: The part of an x-ray tube that either makes the electrons or attracts them.

Electron: The negatively charged part of an atom. When electrons, moving very fast, strike a metal target, x-rays are produced.

Fluoroscope: An x-ray device that uses a chemically coated screen that glows when x-rays hit it. It creates an image of the part of the body being x-rayed.

Isotope: One of two or more atoms of the same element but that has more neutrons in the nucleus than normal. This makes it heavier.

Nuclear radiology or nuclear medicine: Using radioactive substances to create clearer images in radiology. These substances are usually injected into, or swallowed by, the patient before the x-ray is taken.

Radiation: Any rays, wave motion, or particles given off by a radioactive substance. The term usually refers to electromagnetic radiation. Radiation is measured in units called *rads*.

Radioactivity: Unstable atoms that break down, usually producing rays or charged atomic particles.

Radiation sickness: A disease produced by exposure to x-rays or other sources of radiation. Symptoms include diarrhea, vomiting, bleeding, loss of hair, some types of cancer (including leukemia), and sterility.

Radiography: Making a permanent record of the x-ray image on film. The filmed record, often called an x-ray, is technically a radiograph.

Radioisotopes: Radioactive isotopes used to trace nutrients in the body. They emit energy as they decay into nonradioactive substances.

Radiopaque: Describes a material that doesn't let x-rays pass through it.

Tomography: A specialized form of radiology used to study a particular layer of a body part. Layers above or below the part being studied are blurred out so the doctor can get the clearest picture of the part being studied.

Ultrasonic: Sound frequencies above the range of human hearing.

Index

Numbers in *italic* indicate pictures; numbers in **bold** indicate biographies